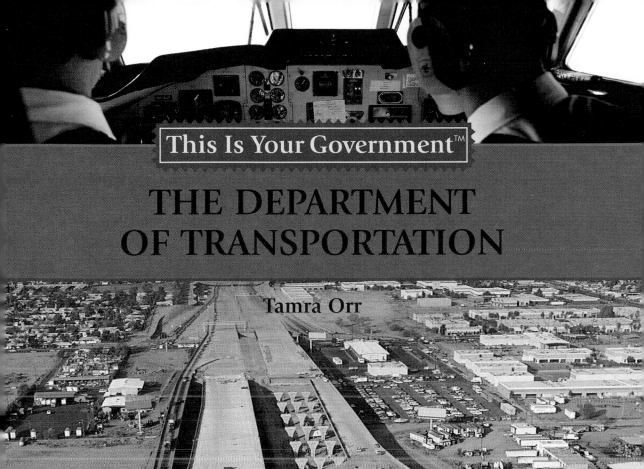

This Is Your Government™

THE DEPARTMENT OF TRANSPORTATION

Tamra Orr

rosen
central™

The Rosen Publishing Group, Inc., New York

Published in 2006 by The Rosen Publishing Group, Inc.
29 East 21st Street, New York, NY 10010

Copyright © 2006 by The Rosen Publishing Group, Inc.

First Edition

Library of Congress Cataloging-in-Publication Data

Orr, Tamra.
The Department of Transportation/by Tamra Orr.
    p. cm.—(This is your government)
Includes bibliographical references and index.
ISBN 1-4042-0211-0 (lib. bdg.)
ISBN 1-4042-0664-7 (pbk. bdg.)
1. United States. Department of Transportation—Juvenile literature.
2. United States. Department of Transportation—History—Juvenile
literature. 3. Transportation—United States—History—Juvenile literature.
I. Title. II. Series.
HE206.3.O77 2005
388'.0973—dc22
                                                    2004003205

Manufactured in the United States of America

Cover images: Left to right: Elizabeth H. Dole, Samuel K. Skinner,
Federico F. Peña, Rodney E. Slater, and Norman Y. Mineta.

CONTENTS

Introduction

Many of the things we use in our daily lives that allow us to get from point A to point B are taken for granted. Roads, bridges, tunnels, trains, buses, and airplanes are just there—maintained and repaired by people we do not see. Travelers and commuters do not think much about these things as they journey on their way.

Behind the scenes, however, the transportation industry is in a constant state of motion and change, as it seeks to improve the safety and efficiency of moving people to their desired destinations. To guard airline passengers from attack, for example, airline and airport security procedures change frequently to keep up with the latest threats. Motor vehicles are constantly being redesigned and upgraded to provide a safer ride. Speed limits are raised or lowered depending on a community's

Department of Transportation Organization Chart

CABINET MEMBERS

| Secretary of Agriculture | Secretary of Commerce | Secretary of Defense | Secretary of Education | Secretary of Energy | Secretary of Health and Human Services | Secretary of Homeland Security | Secretary of Housing and Urban Development |

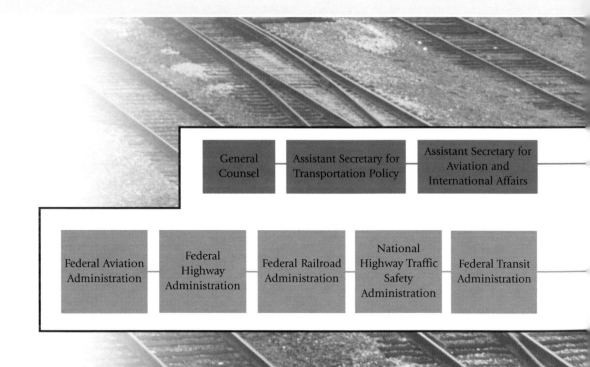

| General Counsel | Assistant Secretary for Transportation Policy | Assistant Secretary for Aviation and International Affairs |

| Federal Aviation Administration | Federal Highway Administration | Federal Railroad Administration | National Highway Traffic Safety Administration | Federal Transit Administration |

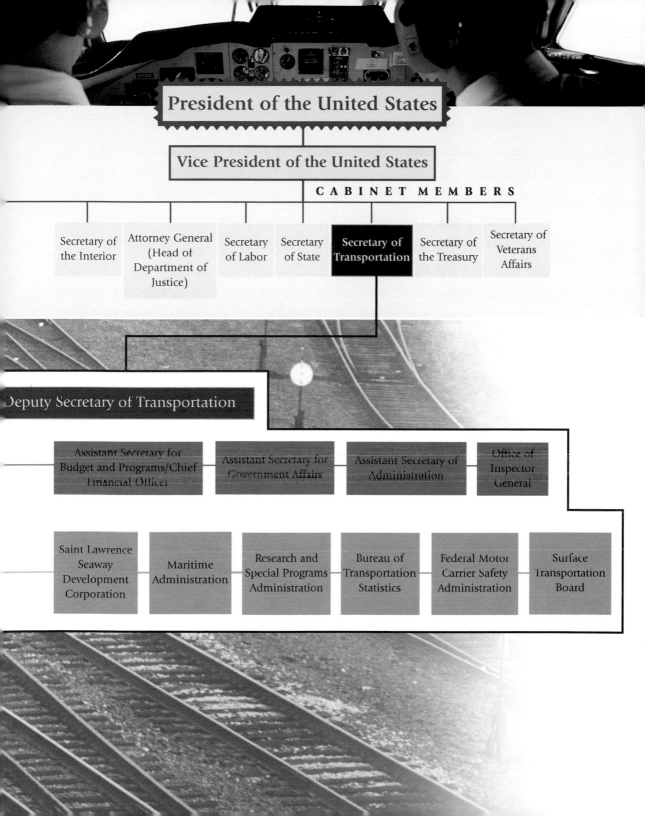

President of the United States

Vice President of the United States

CABINET MEMBERS

| Secretary of the Interior | Attorney General (Head of Department of Justice) | Secretary of Labor | Secretary of State | Secretary of Transportation | Secretary of the Treasury | Secretary of Veterans Affairs |

Deputy Secretary of Transportation

| Assistant Secretary for Budget and Programs/Chief Financial Officer | Assistant Secretary for Government Affairs | Assistant Secretary of Administration | Office of Inspector General |

| Saint Lawrence Seaway Development Corporation | Maritime Administration | Research and Special Programs Administration | Bureau of Transportation Statistics | Federal Motor Carrier Safety Administration | Surface Transportation Board |

competing interests in driver safety or quicker travel. The cargo loaded onto freight trains and ships is examined to ensure that hazardous or illegal materials are not being transported throughout the country. Cities continuously search for new ways to encourage people to take buses, trains, subways, and ferries into and around the city in order to reduce car traffic and pollution.

Thousands of people, millions of miles of roads and oil and natural gas pipelines, and billions of dollars are required to keep the American transportation system up and running every day. It is the job of the Department of Transportation (DOT) to orchestrate and coordinate all of this activity. The DOT is a cabinet-level government office, led by the secretary of transportation. This means that the secretary is directly appointed by the president of the United States, with the advice and consent, or agreement, of the U.S. Congress. Once appointed, the secretary of transportation enters the president's circle of advisers and keeps the president informed on all transportation-related issues. As head of the DOT, the secretary also puts the president's decisions concerning transportation into effect.

The DOT's mission is to develop and coordinate policies that will provide an efficient and affordable national transportation system that carefully balances the needs and interests of travelers and commuters, the environment, and national defense. The DOT is the main government agency that creates and enforces various policies and programs that directly affect how safe, quick, and efficient it is to travel within the United States. If a person hops aboard a train, boards a bus, climbs into a car, gets on an airplane, drives onto a car ferry, or sails on a ship, the DOT had something to do with making that trip possible— from devising safety rules and regulations to installing warning signals and training transportation industry employees.

To help meet this huge responsibility, the DOT has more than 100,000 employees and eleven separate divisions. Most of these divisions handle just one specific mode of transportation (such as trains, planes, or motor vehicles), but there are several that are involved in the entire transportation scene in order to conduct industry-wide research, gather statistics, and create a complete picture of the nation's travel patterns.

The DOT is a government agency that affects every American life in numerous ways. From the newly widened highway passing near town to the extra security scan in the airport, the DOT is there, helping the nation to stay safe and on the move.

CHAPTER ONE

The History of the Department of Transportation

T he Department of Transportation that exists today has been around only since October 15, 1966, when President Lyndon B. Johnson created it by signing the Department of Transportation Act. The idea of such an agency, however, had been around for decades. In the early 1800s, President Thomas Jefferson signed a law that established the first federal highway program, called the National Road. It connected the new state of Ohio with the rest of the eastern seaboard. On January 12, 1874, Representative Laurin D. Woodworth of Ohio introduced a bill that would establish a federal bureau of transportation, but it was not passed by Congress. Throughout the nineteenth century, other legislators

developed an interest in transportation issues, but few nationwide transportation laws were passed.

The Growing Importance of Transportation

At the outset of the twentieth century, as World War I (1914–1918) raged in Europe, President Woodrow Wilson signed the Federal Aid Road Act into law in 1916. This act established the Federal Aid Highway Program, which provided money to the various states for building roads designed mainly for mail delivery. Throughout the 1930s, 1940s, and 1950s, additional programs were created for specific modes of transportation. For example, in 1936, President Franklin Delano Roosevelt signed the Merchant Marine Act, which established the U.S. Maritime Commission, a forerunner of the Maritime Administration. In 1956, the National System of Interstate and Defense Highways was set up. Two years later, the Federal Aviation Agency (FAA) was created.

In the summer of 1961, the U.S. Senate Committee on Commerce published a report that called for the creation of a new Department of Transportation that would oversee and regulate all of the nation's various forms of transportation. The president at the time, John F. Kennedy, responded to this proposal by instead establishing an Office of Transportation within the Housing and House Finance Agency.

The idea for an independent, powerful, cabinet-level transportation department would not go away, however. In 1965, the Federal Aviation Agency administrator under President

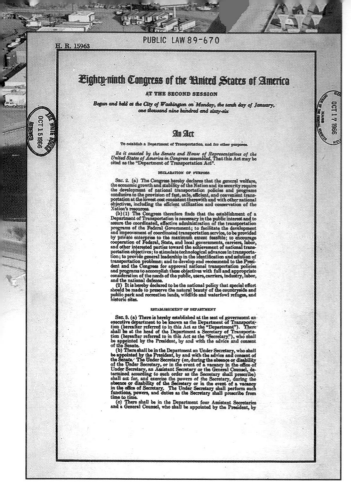

Public Law 89-670, better known as the Department of Transportation Act *(left)*, was signed into law on October 15, 1966. The new cabinet-level department began operation on April 1, 1967. The act charges the department with providing "fast, safe, efficient, and convenient transportation at the lowest cost," while ensuring "efficient utilization and conservation of the Nation's resources."

Lyndon B. Johnson, Najeeb E. Halaby, recommended the establishment of just such a department, of which the FAA would become a part. In his State of the Union speech in January 1966, Johnson publicly stated that he planned to establish a DOT during his administration. In March, a bill was sent to Congress stating that "in a nation that spans a continent, transportation is the web of union" and that a federal transportation department was therefore necessary.

The Birth of the DOT

Finally, on October 15, 1966, Johnson signed Public Law 89-670, at last establishing the Department of Transportation. Less than a month later, Alan Boyd was named the nation's first secretary of transportation. He stated that the new agency would be committed to making transportation faster, more efficient, more economical, and more socially responsible.

New transportation policies and ideas were developed very quickly under Secretary Boyd's leadership. In January 1967, the DOT issued its first twenty federal motor vehicle safety standards. In March, the first National Highway Safety Advisory committee was formed. By April 1, Secretary Boyd had brought under one roof more than thirty transportation agencies and functions scattered throughout the government, and about 95,000 employees, most of whom had previously been working for the Federal Aviation Agency, the Coast Guard, and the Bureau of Public Roads.

By the end of Secretary Boyd's term in 1969, the DOT had grown to include the Coast Guard, the newly renamed Federal Aviation Administration, the Federal Highway Administration, the Federal Railroad Administration, the Saint Lawrence Seaway Development Corporation, the Urban Mass Transportation Administration, and the National Transportation Safety Board. Boyd's greatest achievement as secretary was to organize the DOT and get it operating smoothly.

Confronting Grave Challenges

The former governor of Massachusetts, John Volpe, succeeded Boyd as secretary of transportation under President Richard M.

Eleven years after a brief work stoppage during Secretary John Volpe's tenure, air traffic controllers again walked off the job on August 3, 1981 *(above)*. The controllers' union—PATCO—was holding out for higher wages, a shorter workweek, and a better retirement package. On August 5, President Ronald Reagan fired the nearly 13,000 strikers, roughly three-quarters of the nation's air traffic controllers.

Nixon. During Secretary Volpe's term, the DOT was forced to confront a number of national transportation problems. Airlines were occasionally being taken over by terrorists who took passengers hostage and hijacked planes to other countries. Hundreds of members of the Professional Air Traffic Controllers Organization (PATCO) had gone on strike. The Penn Central Railroad had declared bankruptcy.

In response to these new developments, the DOT transformed national transportation policy. It headed the government's anti-hijacking program and instituted mandatory pre-boarding electronic scanning of airline passengers and inspection of their carry-on luggage. It recommended allowing air traffic controllers to retire with full benefits after twenty-five years of active service. The DOT also helped to set up American Travel and Track, or Amtrak, a new intercity national passenger train service that would take over and expand many of Penn Central's routes.

When Nixon resigned the presidency in 1974, and was replaced by his vice president, Gerald R. Ford, William T. Coleman Jr. became the new secretary of transportation. Coleman created several reports during his brief time in office that focused on current and future transportation trends and the decisions that had to be made in order to ensure the continued health and vitality of the nation's transportation system. Some of the DOT's most important policies under Coleman included instituting a national fifty-five-mile-per-hour (eighty-nine-kilometer-per-hour) speed limit on a permanent basis, encouraging carpooling (several people riding to work together in a single car), and making funds available for the resurfacing and restoring of the nation's interstate highways.

The DOT Changes Shape

Following his defeat of Ford in the 1976 presidential election, Jimmy Carter appointed Brock Adams as secretary of trans-portation. Adams made a major change in the structure of the

DOT when he created the Research and Special Programs Administration (RSPA), a gathering of transportation agencies that did not comfortably fit into any of the DOT's other existing agencies. Included in the RSPA were the Transportation Systems Center and safety programs related to hazardous material transportation and oil and gas pipelines. This was the first DOT division to have been created by the department secretary rather than Congress. Secretary Adams also recommended that the Federal Highway Administration and the Urban Mass Transportation Administration be reorganized into the Surface Transportation Board, combining federal assistance programs for the nation's highways and its cities' public transportation systems.

Near the end of his term, President Carter reshuffled his cabinet in advance of the 1980 presidential election. Adams was replaced as secretary of transportation by Neil Goldschmidt, a former mayor of Portland, Oregon. Under Secretary Goldschmidt, the department oversaw a number of deregulation acts—laws that loosened the government's rules about transportation, encouraging competition between transportation companies and lower prices for their passengers. In a short period of time, the Railroad Regulatory Act, the Truck Regulatory Reform Act, the International Airlines Reform Act, and the Household Goods Regulatory Reform Act were all passed.

The Reagan and Bush Years

President Ronald Reagan served as president of the United States throughout most of the 1980s. The first transportation secretary he appointed was Andrew L. Lewis Jr., a management consultant and political leader. Like Secretary Volpe, Lewis had to deal with another strike by PATCO members. In negotiations, he took a hard-line position with the air traffic controllers, saying that those who did not return to work would lose their jobs. He was backed in his statements by the president. When the striking workers refused to return to work, most of the nation's air traffic controllers were fired and replaced. The strikers were never allowed to work as controllers again.

Lewis's successor, still serving under Reagan, was Elizabeth H. Dole, the first woman to serve as secretary of transportation. Her main focus was on making car travel safer. To this end, Dole tried to educate the public on the dangers of drunk driving. She also urged automakers to adopt so-called passive restraint systems, such as air bags and automatic seat belts, in their cars.

President Reagan was succeeded in 1989 by George H. W. Bush. Bush chose Samuel K. Skinner as his secretary of transportation. Secretary Skinner's main goal was to create a national policy that would maintain and expand the nation's transportation system and encourage the technologies that would create a first-class transportation system in the twenty-first century. Above all, Skinner wanted to oversee a transportation system that would protect the safety of American citizens, the environment, and the economy, while also promoting national security.

As part of this effort, the DOT restructured its highway, highway safety, and transit programs. Two new groups were also established within the DOT. The first of these, the Bureau of Transportation Statistics, collects, studies, and publishes transportation statistics. The second, the Office of Intermodalism, develops and coordinates federal policy on intermodal transportation, or the use of two or more kinds of transportation during a single journey.

Secretary Skinner also wanted the DOT to increase its role in disaster response. During his time in office, there was no shortage of disasters and crises affecting American transportation to respond to: the terrorist attack on Pan Am Flight 103 in December 1988, the *Exxon Valdez* oil spill in March 1989, the Loma Prieta earthquake in California in October 1989, the arrival of Hurricane Hugo in September 1990, and the Gulf War of 1991.

A New Plan

Following his defeat of George H. W. Bush in the 1992 presidential election, Bill Clinton appointed Federico F. Peña as his secretary of transportation. As part of a larger, government-wide

THE DEPARTMENT OF TRANSPORTATION AT WORK: THE HIGHWAY-RAIL CROSSING SAFETY AND TRESPASS PREVENTION PROGRAM

The Federal Railroad Administration's Highway-Rail Crossing Safety and Trespass Prevention Program is committed to reducing the number of car-train collisions at rail crossings, where approximately 900 deaths occur every year. Using the "Three E's"—education, enforcement, and engineering—the program has helped reduce the number of deaths at highway-rail crossings by 43 percent since 1994. Education involves going into schools and workplaces in communities across the country to teach about rail safety. Enforcement involves making sure that railroad employees, car drivers, and pedestrians alike obey and respect the rules governing safety on and near train tracks. The development of new technology—engineering—such as various high-tech rail barriers or train detection devices, also helps the Federal Railroad Administration save lives.

Emergency workers respond at the scene of a collision between a freight train and a pickup truck near Blairstown, Iowa, in 2003.

19

attempt to improve the quality and reduce the cost of government services, Secretary Peña drafted the DOT Strategic Plan in January 1994. The plan outlined the department's mission and stated several goals for the coming years: to knit America together through an effective intermodal transportation system, to upgrade and improve transportation infrastructure (such as bridges, tunnels, airports, and highways), to promote safe and secure transportation, and to put people and the environment ahead of industry when making important transportation decisions.

As always, driver safety remained one of the DOT's chief concerns under Secretary Peña. Drug and alcohol testing guidelines for transportation industry employees were finalized in 1994. In addition, several educational programs were launched. For example, Share the Road taught motorists how to drive in areas heavily traveled by commercial trucks. Another program, Always Expect a Train, educated drivers about the severe consequences of collisions with trains at rail crossings.

Terror and Transportation

Norman Y. Mineta, President Clinton's secretary of commerce, switched cabinet positions in 2001, when President George W. Bush asked him to head the DOT. Only eight months after Mineta took office, on September 11, 2001, Al Qaeda terrorists hijacked four American commercial jets and used three of them as missiles to strike the World Trade Center in New York City and the Pentagon in Arlington, Virginia. Over 3,000 people were killed in these buildings and on the airplanes, including the fourth plane that crashed in Shanksville, Pennsylvania, before it could reach the hijackers' intended target. As it became clear that terrorists were using the nation's jets as weapons, hundreds of DOT employees had to call upon their many years of planning, training, and education in order to direct the safe grounding of every single aircraft flying in American airspace at the time of the attacks.

In the immediate wake of the September 11 attacks, President Bush signed into law the Aviation and Transportation Security Act, calling for increased security, not only in airports but also in other major transportation centers, such as seaports and train stations. Within the DOT, a new Transportation and Security Administration was created to increase and monitor security at important transportation sites. A year later, the cabinet-level Department of Homeland Security was created. It was designed to coordinate all of the nation's domestic security efforts and gathered together in one department many security-related agencies scattered throughout the federal government. As part of this consolidation, the DOT transferred the Transportation and Security Administration and the Coast Guard to this new cabinet office.

Though the Department of Homeland Security is spearheading the nation's efforts to protect itself against enemy attacks, the Department of Transportation remains as committed

New York City police officers ride a subway in order to protect against terrorist acts and reassure riders of public transportation safety. Following the terrorist attacks on New York's World Trade Center on September 11, 2001, the city beefed up patrols in subways, subway stations, train stations, ferries, ferry terminals, tunnels, bridges, shopping districts, and other sensitive or vulnerable locations.

as ever to protecting Americans as they travel throughout the country and overseas. Whether the dangers be excessive speeding, poorly maintained highways, the unsafe transportation of hazardous goods, or terrorist attacks, the DOT is always working to find ways to make getting where we want to go more pleasant and, most important, more safe.

CHAPTER TWO

The Secretaries of Transportation

Over the course of the forty years between its start and 2003, the Department of Transportation has had a total of fourteen leaders. The role of the secretary is an important one. The appointed leader must supervise the creation of national transportation policy. He or she is also responsible for negotiating and putting in place international transportation agreements, ensuring the safety of U.S. airlines, and enforcing airline consumer protection regulations. The secretary of transportation also issues regulations to prevent alcohol and illegal drug use by transportation industry employees (such as pilots, train engineers, and air traffic controllers) and develops new transportation laws. In addition to this, the secretary oversees an agency that has more than 100,000 employees and a budget of almost $60 billion. Let's

take a closer look at some of the men and women who have shouldered this great responsibility.

Alan S. Boyd (1967–1969)

The very first person to have the title of secretary of transportation was a man named Alan Stephenson Boyd. When appointed by President Lyndon B. Johnson in 1967, Boyd had already gained extensive experience in transportation. Not only was he the former Civil Aeronautics Board chairman and undersecretary of commerce for transportation, he had also served as the chairman of the Florida Railroad and Public Utilities Commission. Secretary Boyd was faced with a different kind of challenge in his new job, however. This time, he was in charge of creating a brand-new cabinet-level department, building it from scratch while paying careful attention to Congress's recommendations.

During Boyd's two years in office, the department issued the very first national safety and federal motor vehicle standards. President Johnson increased the secretary's responsibilities when he transferred the Urban Mass Transportation Administration from the Department of Housing and Urban Development to the newly formed DOT. In addition to this, Boyd also concentrated on modernizing airports and updating air traffic control requirements. By shaping the new DOT and establishing its responsibilities and standards, Secretary Boyd created a road map for those who would follow in his footsteps as leader of this important department.

After Secretary Boyd left the DOT, he remained within the transportation industry, first becoming the president of the Illinois Central Railroad and then the president of Amtrak. Later, he became the chairman of Airbus Industries of North America, a manufacturer of passenger aircraft.

Dr. Claude Stout Brinegar (1973–1975)

The third secretary of transportation was a forty-five-year-old man named Claude Stout Brinegar. He approached the position with a strong background in business and economics. He had served as the senior vice president of the Union Oil Company, a California-based oil company. He also held a Ph.D. in economic research from Stanford University.

During his term, Brinegar was confronted with the energy crisis of 1973 to 1974, which was caused by an oil embargo imposed on the United States by the Arab-dominated Organization of Petroleum Exporting Countries (OPEC). The Arab nations in OPEC were angered at the United States for its support of Israel during the 1973 Yom Kippur War, in which Israel beat back a surprise attack led by Egypt and Syria. The result was a severe shortage of the imported oil and gas on which the United States heavily relies. The energy crisis called the nation's attention to the impact of transportation—especially car travel—on energy consumption.

In response to the energy crisis, President Nixon and Secretary Brinegar put into place several new pieces of transportation and

In 1974, in the wake of the OPEC oil embargo, the federal government imposed the 55-mile-per-hour (89 km/h) National Maximum Speed Limit (NMSL) on American drivers in an effort to conserve gas. The slower speeds also resulted in a reduction in highway deaths. Yet the national speed limit was unpopular with many people, and efforts to repeal it were common. Above, supporters of the national speed limit legislation rally outside the Capitol in Washington, D.C., in 1987. In 1995, the national speed limit was repealed, and states were allowed to set their own speed limits.

energy policy. Nixon launched Project Independence, which called for American energy self-sufficiency by 1980. As part of this effort, Nixon authorized the construction of an oil pipeline that would carry 2 million barrels of crude oil from Alaska's northern oil fields to its ice-free port of Valdez for shipment to the continental United States. The president also instituted an emergency fifteen-month daylight savings period (from January 1974 through April 1975), designed to cut energy use by prolonging the daylight into the evening hours. Together, Nixon and Brinegar promoted carpooling and first instituted the national 55-mile-per-hour speed limit (89 km/h), which helped reduce fuel use.

Following President Nixon's resignation, Secretary Brinegar stepped down and returned to his job at Union Oil.

Brockman "Brock" Adams (1977–1979)

When President Jimmy Carter appointed Brockman Adams to the position of secretary of transportation, he chose someone with a high degree of political experience. Adams had already served six terms in the House of Representatives from the state of Washington, and there had been rumors that he was a strong candidate for the job of Speaker of the House. During his years in the House, Adams was considered to be an authority on transportation issues. He had been the principal author of the legislation that had taken the bankrupt northeastern rail lines and converted them into the profitable Conrail system.

In his two years with the DOT, Adams had a major impact on the safety designs of motor vehicles. Through his dedication, air bags and automated seat belts started to move from the idea stage toward their eventual installation in every car manufactured in the United States. He announced new fuel economy standards and demanded that automobile manufacturers make design changes that would result in smaller, lighter cars that would use less fuel per mile driven. Following his time at the DOT, Adams went on to serve in the U.S. Senate, representing Washington State from 1987 to 1993.

Elizabeth Hanford Dole (1983–1987)

President Ronald Reagan appointed Elizabeth Hanford Dole to be the eighth secretary of the DOT. By the time she reached this position, she had already gained quite a bit of experience in the government. In the 1960s, she headed the White House's Office of Consumer Affairs. From 1973 to 1979, she served as the commissioner of the Federal Trade Commission under presidents Nixon, Ford, and Carter. After serving as Reagan's assistant for public liaison for three years, he appointed her to the DOT. She was the first woman ever to hold this position.

Dole spent her two terms as secretary focusing on many safety-related issues, especially air bag usage. She helped establish deadlines for installing these safety devices in vehicles and created a variety of incentives to encourage motor vehicle manufacturers to equip cars with these life-saving bags. In addition, she emphasized increasing seat belt usage by the general public and encouraged individual states to pass laws requiring them. Perhaps she is best known, however, for what came to be called the "Dole brake light." It was her idea and her efforts that resulted in rear-window brake lights being installed in various motor vehicles starting in the mid-1980s.

After leaving the department, Dole continued in politics. She supported her husband, Bob Dole, during his unsuccessful 1996 presidential election campaign. Later, she served as President Bush's secretary of labor and then as the president of

THE DEPARTMENT OF TRANSPORTATION AT WORK: THE NEW CAR ASSESSMENT PROGRAM

In 1978, the National Highway Traffic Safety Administration began its New Car Assessment Program. This program was designed to give car buyers reliable information about how safe specific models of cars were. In order to provide this information, the program ran a series of front- and side-crash tests on many of the cars sold in the United States. The results of the program's crash tests also often encourage automakers to make safer cars, if only so they will not receive the bad publicity that comes with having a car fail the test. The vehicles chosen for the crash tests are new models that are expected to be sold in great numbers and those that have been redesigned or have received new safety features. For testing frontal collisions, crash-test dummies are placed in driver and front passenger seats and wear seat belts.

(continued on next page)

As part of the New Car Assessment Program, a worker from the National Highway Traffic Safety Administration examines the results of a crash test. The program's crash tests are designed to gather and publish information concerning the safety of specific vehicles in front and side collisions.

THE DEPARTMENT OF TRANSPORTATION AT WORK: THE NEW CAR ASSESSMENT PROGRAM

(continued from previous page)

Vehicles are crashed into a fixed barrier at 35 miles per hour (56 km/h), which is equivalent to a head-on collision between two similar vehicles each moving at 35 miles per hour. Instruments measure the force of impact to each dummy's head, chest, and legs. The resulting information indicates a belted person's chances of suffering a serious injury in the event of a crash. For testing side-impact collisions, crash-test dummies are placed in driver and driver's side rear passenger seats wearing seat belts. This test represents an intersection-type collision with a 3,015-pound (1,368-kilogram) barrier moving at 38.5 miles per hour (62 km/h) into a standing vehicle.

the American Red Cross. In 2001, she campaigned successfully to succeed North Carolina's retiring senator, Jesse Helms.

Norman Yoshio Mineta (2001–present)

On January 25, 2001, Norman Yoshio Mineta became the fourteenth U.S. secretary of transportation, serving under President George W. Bush. Previous to his nomination, he had been the U.S. secretary of commerce under President Bill Clinton, the first Japanese American ever to serve in the cabinet. For twenty years (1975–1995), Mineta was a member of the U.S. House of Representatives, serving California's Silicon

Secretary of Transportation Norman Mineta delivers a speech calling for new transportation investments on December 15, 2003, in Little Rock, Arkansas. He is surrounded by highway construction workers who would benefit from any new funds spent on highways and mass transit.

Valley (an international headquarters for computer technology), where he specialized in a number of transportation issues. These included investing in infrastructure, encouraging efficient intermodal transportation, and boosting mass transit ridership and environmentally friendly transportation alternatives.

As a boy, Mineta had been one of the 120,000 Japanese Americans who were forced out of their homes and into internment camps during World War II (1939–1945). At the time, the government feared that the loyalties of Japanese Americans might rest with Japan rather than the United States. In order to prevent any spying or sabotage, the government ordered these citizens to be rounded up and virtually imprisoned—a violation of their rights as Americans—despite their innocence and lack of any formal charges of wrongdoing. In response to his wartime experiences in internment camp, Mineta became a driving force behind

HR 442, the Civil Liberties Act of 1988, while serving in the House. This act, which was passed by Congress and signed by President Reagan, was an official government apology for the injustices committed against the Japanese Americans. For his efforts on behalf of this act, Mineta was awarded the Martin Luther King Jr. Commemorative Medal.

Mineta was serving as secretary of transportation when the World Trade Center and the Pentagon were attacked on September 11, 2001, by terrorists flying hijacked American airplanes. On that day, Mineta, along with DOT managers and air traffic controllers, performed the enormous task of bringing every airplane flying in American airspace at the time of the attacks back down to the ground safely. The entire nation's aviation system was shut down in less than two hours.

In the wake of September 11, Mineta's job and the DOT's responsibilities increased greatly. The secretary helped draft the new Aviation and Transportation Security Act, a law designed to strengthen security throughout the country's airports. Under the terms of this law, Mineta helped create the Transportation Security Administration, which was initially housed within the DOT. It was later transferred to the newly created Department of Homeland Security. Mineta stayed on as DOT secretary in George W. Bush's second presidential administration.

CHAPTER THREE

How the Department of Transportation Works

The Department of Transportation is divided into eleven principal agencies. Each one has very specific responsibilities that set it apart from the other ten agencies, though there is occasional overlap. The secretary of transportation, working within the Office of the Secretary of Transportation, acts as the head of each DOT agency and reports directly to the president of the United States. The secretary also oversees new policies for every agency. This includes negotiating and putting into place international transportation agreements, enforcing consumer protection regulations, and preparing upcoming transportation-related legislation. It is an immense job, and the secretary is assisted in it by a deputy secretary.

The eleven primary DOT agencies are the Bureau of Transportation Statistics, the Federal Aviation Administration, the Federal Highway Administration, the Federal Motor Carrier Safety Administration, the Federal Railroad Administration, the Federal Transit Administration, the Maritime Administration, the National Highway Traffic Safety Administration, the Research and Special Programs Administration, the Saint Lawrence Seaway Development Corporation, and the Surface Transportation Board. Up until the September 11 terrorist attacks, the DOT had two additional divisions: the United States Coast Guard and the Transportation Security Administration. These divisions were transferred to the Department of Homeland Security when that office was created in 2002 in response to the attacks.

Bureau of Transportation Statistics (BTS)

Just as its name implies, the Bureau of Transportation Statistics (BTS) focuses on compiling and analyzing various statistics regarding the nation's different forms of transportation. It collects enormous amounts of data, or facts and figures, and publishes the information in order to educate politicians and the public about potential decisions relating to transportation issues. Along with the Bureau of the Census, the BTS also helps identify exactly where freight and people travel and by what mode of transportation. For this reason, unlike many of the other divisions of the DOT, the BTS is concerned with all kinds of transportation, rather than just one.

An air traffic controller demonstrates a state-of-the-art ground radar system in the new air traffic control tower at Chicago's O'Hare International Airport in 1996. At the time, the 260-foot (79.24-meter) tower was the largest ever built by the FAA.

Federal Aviation Administration (FAA)

The FAA is responsible for the safety of civil aviation, or planes that nonmilitary passengers fly. The division was created in 1958 under the name of the Federal Aviation Agency, and became the Federal Aviation Administration when it joined the DOT in 1967.

The FAA enforces the regulations and minimum standards relating to the production, operation, and maintenance of aircraft. In addition to drafting the rules governing air traffic, the FAA controls the nation's air traffic by maintaining and supervising a network of airport towers, air route traffic control centers, and flight service stations. It builds and installs equipment that makes flying safer and easier, such as radar facilities, voice and data communications equipment, and computer systems. The FAA also exchanges aeronautical information with its counterparts in other countries.

The FAA has a division dedicated to research, engineering, and development. Through this division, the FAA develops better aircraft and engines and tests and evaluates new flight materials and procedures. The FAA registers all aircraft based in the United States, develops specifications for aeronautical charts, and publishes information on various topics within aeronautics. The administration provides a great deal of information to citizens, including details about traveling with a disability, airport and flight delays, security tips, and more.

Federal Highway Administration (FHWA)

Not only does the Federal Highway Administration ensure that federal highways, roads, bridges, and tunnels stay safe, it also helps repair things when disaster strikes. Whether earthquakes shatter the roads or floods engulf them, for example, the FHWA arrives on the scene in order to make emergency repairs. The FHWA has two basic programs. First, there is the Federal-Aid Highway Program, which focuses on providing federal funds to the states in order to build and improve the National Highway System, as well as urban and rural roads and bridges. The FHWA's Federal Lands Highway Program provides access to places like Native American reservations, national forests and parks, and other public lands.

In the aftermath of Hurricane Isabel, which struck the East Coast of the United States in September 2003, a front-end loader operated by the Maryland State Highway Administration clears fallen tree limbs from State Route 77. The DOT's Federal Emergency Relief Program provides funds for the repair or reconstruction of federal-aid highways damaged by natural disasters or other catastrophic accidents. In addition, the department's Federal Highway Administration can allow states to redirect existing highway money to pay for transportation recovery and reconstruction efforts.

Federal Motor Carrier Safety Administration (FMCSA)

The FMCSA is a relative newcomer to the DOT, having been established in January 2000. Its primary aim is to do everything it can to decrease the number of accidents and injuries from crashes involving motor carriers—trucks or buses. In order to do this, the FMCSA creates and enforces federal rules that govern carrier safety. It establishes safe operating requirements for professional truck drivers, their vehicles, and their equipment.

In addition, the FMCSA enforces rules that try to ensure the safe transport of hazardous materials from one place to another.

To ensure that bus and truck drivers in the United States are properly trained and educated, the FMCSA administers both the Commercial Driver's License Program and the New Entrant Safety Assurance Process. It also sponsors a federal grant program called the Motor Carrier Safety Assistance Program, which supplies the states with the financial assistance they need in order to conduct roadside inspections of trucks and buses as well as reviews of driver performance and licensing. The Performance and Registration Information Systems Management is another FMCSA program that monitors the safety records of carriers and their drivers.

Other FMCSA programs include the Motor Carrier Safety Identification and Information Systems, which gathers data about national crash statistics. A Research and Technology division develops new methods to improve truck safety. The Border and International Safety division works with the governments of Canada and Mexico to make sure that their drivers meet the appropriate safety standards before they enter the United States.

Federal Railroad Administration (FRA)

The FRA was first established in 1966 in order to ensure and improve the safety of railroads through both the maintenance of the nation's train tracks and trains, and the education of rail industry employees. FRA safety inspectors make sure that rail

THE DEPARTMENT OF TRANSPORTATION AT WORK: DRIVER ALERTNESS AND FATIGUE RESEARCH AND TECHNOLOGY

Through its Driver Alertness and Fatigue Research and Technology division, the Federal Motor Carrier Safety Administration has sponsored numerous studies on the dangerous effects of tiredness on truck drivers. The largest of these identified several important problems. Driver alertness and safe driving had more to do with the time of day than with how many hours the driver had been on the road. Drowsiness was eight times more likely between midnight and 6 AM than during other times of the day. In addition, most drivers involved in the study slept only five hours a day, two hours less than is ideal. Drivers were also often found to be poor judges of their ability to drive safely. The way drivers said they felt often contradicted how well they drove. The study involved eighty drivers and more than 200,000 miles (321,869 km) of highway driving. Numerous measurements were taken of the drivers' alertness and performance during driving and of their physical and mental functions during off-duty sleep periods. The results of this and similar studies are helping the Federal Highway Administration to revise its regulations concerning the trucking industry and its driving practices and will lead to safer highways in the future.

With increasing rail use in the United States, the importance of track maintenance becomes ever more important if serious accidents, derailments, injuries, and fatalities are to be avoided. In addition to maintenance, the DOT invests in safety programs and new technologies.

companies are obeying federally established rail safety standards. In addition, research and development tests are used to enhance the rail system as a national transportation resource. For example, the so-called bullet trains—trains that can travel at speeds greater than 100 miles per hour (161 km/h)—are the sort of new technology being carefully studied by the FRA. The administration also leads public education campaigns designed to warn against the extreme dangers of driving across rail crossings or walking along train tracks.

Federal Transit Administration (FTA)

The FTA's mission is to develop and improve systems of mass transit for cities nationwide. Mass transit refers to the systems of vehicles—trains, subways, buses, ferries—that carry large groups of people to and throughout large cities. The FTA's staff helps to plan, build, and operate these systems and place an emphasis on passenger affordability, accessibility, and convenience.

Detailed data and records are kept on each mode of mass transit. This information is shared with those who must make transit decisions, such as whether to expand bus lines or add subway cars based on heavy ridership.

Maritime Administration (MARAD)

MARAD is mainly concerned with promoting the development of a strong U.S. merchant marine. The merchant marine is simply all of the nation's commercial, nonmilitary ships that are used to carry goods on the United States' oceans, rivers, and lakes. In times of war or other national emergency, the merchant marine may be called upon to assist the armed forces by lending its boats and crews for military purposes, such as the transport of equipment or soldiers. MARAD also ensures that the United States maintains enough shipbuilding and repair services, efficient ports, effective water and land transportation systems, and reserve ships for use in any national emergencies.

National Highway Traffic Safety Administration (NHTSA)

Established in 1970, the NHTSA is the primary DOT division responsible for reducing the deaths, injuries, and economic losses that often accompany motor vehicle crashes. It carries out this mission by setting and enforcing safety performance standards for motor vehicle equipment and offering grants to state and local governments for the development and installation of local highway safety programs.

41

Investigators inspect and photograph the scene of a fatal two-car crash in York County, Pennsylvania, in December 2002. Since 1972, the Special Crash Investigations (SCI) Program of the National Highway Traffic Safety Administration (NHTSA) has collected and analyzed crash scene data in order to detect vehicle defects and study the impact of new technology— such as seat belts, air bags, and alternative fuels—on traffic safety. The data collected range from basic data maintained in routine police and insurance crash reports to comprehensive data from special reports by professional crash investigation teams.

The NHTSA also investigates safety defects in vehicles and enforces fuel economy standards (how many miles per gallon of gas a car can drive). The NHTSA helps communities keep drunk drivers off the road, promotes the use of seat belts and child safety seats, and provides important safety information to consumers about traffic issues. This is the department that issues recalls when something is found to be wrong with a vehicle. It also performs crash tests on all types of vehicles to learn how

When cargo containers like the one pictured here arrive in port aboard freighters, they are unloaded and transferred onto barges, freight trains, or trucks for the next stage of their journey toward their ultimate destination—the consumer marketplace.

they fare in an accident. The results of these tests are published, offering car buyers valuable information about which cars are the safest.

Research and Special Programs Administration (RSPA)

The RSPA has been in existence since 1977 and was initially designed to administer the programs that did not easily fit into the other DOT divisions. Today, the RSPA focuses primarily on developing new technology that will improve the safety and efficiency with which people and cargo are transported throughout the entire world using all available forms of transportation. As part of this mission, the RSPA is charged with reducing the risk of the transportation of hazardous goods, such as the shipping of toxic chemicals in tanker trucks or the delivery of oil through pipelines. By offering training and technical assistance, the RSPA also makes sure that communities are prepared for any transportation-related emergencies that may occur, such as a chemical spill on a local highway.

Saint Lawrence Seaway Development Corporation (SLSDC)

The SLSDC works together with the Saint Lawrence Seaway Authority of Canada to provide safe and efficient passage for commercial and noncommercial ships traveling throughout the Great Lakes and along the Saint Lawrence Seaway to or from the Atlantic Ocean. This waterway is 2,342 miles (3,769 km) long and includes canals, dams, and locks in the Saint Lawrence River, along with connecting channels between the Great Lakes. The Saint Lawrence Seaway formally opened in 1959. The SLSDC is responsible for operations safety, vessel inspections, traffic control, and navigation aids along the Saint Lawrence Seaway. It also helps develop trade opportunities that benefit everyone involved in seaway trade, from ports and shippers to receivers and consumers.

Surface Transportation Board (STB)

Established in 1996, the STB is responsible for making sure that the transportation services provided by railroads, certain trucking and moving companies, intercity buses, and ocean shipping companies are both safe and fairly priced. Although it is housed within the DOT, it is considered independent.

44

CHAPTER FOUR

The Department of Transportation in the Twenty-first Century

As the United States' population continues to grow and its people and goods continue to be so mobile, transportation problems are bound to increase, despite the best efforts of the DOT. Hoping to anticipate the nation's twenty-first century transportation needs and problems, DOT inventors, researchers, and scientists have studied America's likely future and formed some possible strategies and solutions. While some of their ideas may seem like they were taken directly from the pages of science-fiction novels, they all are based in reality. With each passing year, these futuristic scenarios are becoming more and more likely.

Planes

The future of flight will be determined by what new planes can be made to do and what new materials will go into their construction. Scientists at the Langley Research Center in Virginia have been working on a program they call the Morphing Project. To morph is to undergo a major change of some kind. Early studies in this project are focusing on a new kind of material that would be used in the construction of airplane wings. This high-tech material would allow the wings to flex or bend on command, detect changes in pressure, and even shift from a liquid to a solid when placed in a magnetic field in order to bend into a new shape or repair damage to its structure. Because the material would allow them to be fully adjustable, the wings would not have any mechanical flaps, which would save fuel and money.

Trains

Train designs will also be undergoing a number of changes. A new type of train being tested in Britain tilts as it goes around corners, keeping it fully upright and level no matter how steeply the ground beneath it slopes. This allows the train to maintain speeds of about 140 miles per hour (225 km/h) even when it is not traveling on a straight stretch of track.

Another new train design that is creating a lot of interest and enthusiasm is the maglev train, or magnetic levitation train. Instead of cars outfitted with steel wheels that ride on

An experimental model maglev (magnetic levitation) train runs on an 11.4-mile (18.4 km) test track in Tsuru, west of Tokyo, Japan, in November 2003. The maglev train can go from 0 to 310 mph (500 km/h) in less than ninety seconds.

the tracks, the maglev train features magnets under its cars. A magnetic field created by magnetized coils in the guideway— the maglev equivalent of train tracks—floats the train above the ground and pushes and pulls it along at very high speeds. In some trials, maglev trains have ranged between 260 and 340 miles per hour (418 and 547 km/h). Because there are no wheels making contact with the track, there is no friction to slow the train down or require a large, fossil fuel–burning engine. In fact, the magnetic field powers the train, so there is no need for either fuel or an engine on a maglev train. Already, the DOT has given millions of dollars to seven different companies to try to develop the best system for America's needs.

THE DEPARTMENT OF TRANSPORTATION AT WORK: THE PEDESTRIAN AND BICYCLIST SAFETY PROGRAM

Pedestrian and bicyclist deaths represent about 15 percent of all roadway-related deaths each year. For this reason, the Federal Highway Administration sponsors the Pedestrian and Bicyclist Safety Program, which is designed to reduce these deaths. In specific locations that have been proven dangerous to walkers and bike riders, the program recommends that public officials make certain changes to fix the problem.

For example, in an area known for its pedestrian and bicyclist deaths, representatives of the Pedestrian and Bicyclist Safety Program might recommend the building of sidewalks, the installation of street lamps, and the addition of crosswalks and traffic lights. They may also urge pedestrians and bicyclists to wear bright or reflective clothing when walking and riding after dark. In addition, the Federal Highway Administration has joined forces with the National Highway Traffic Safety Administration to develop a new pedestrian program called the Pedestrian Safety Roadshow. This program is designed to help communities identify and solve their own problems related to local pedestrian safety.

Cars

Perhaps the transportation mode that will require the most attention and creative problem solving in the coming years will be motor vehicles. Traffic congestion worsens from year to year. Each year, American commuters collectively spend 5 billion hours sitting in rush-hour traffic jams. It is estimated that the average rush hour driver spends sixty-two hours a year sitting in stalled traffic. While the solution once seemed simple—build more roads—there is no longer enough room left to do that. Instead, researchers at the DOT and other organizations are trying to find ways to make the most of the highways that already exist and to encourage commuters to take advantage of the mass transit and carpooling opportunities that are already available to them.

When it comes to applying the latest technological advances to America's roads, the ideas are almost limitless. Most of them revolve around designing cars and road systems that work in a completely different way from what people are used to. For example, one possibility is installing magnetometers inside cars that would be controlled by magnets embedded in the roads. The magnetometers would help control the speed and steering of vehicles, thereby regulating traffic flow. Similar to this is the concept of visual sensors inside cars that communicate with special highway marking tapes warning drivers to slow down or advising them when it is safe to change lanes.

Two specially equipped Honda Accords drive down a 7.6-mile (12.2 km) stretch of Interstate 15 in San Diego, California, in July 1997. Magnetic sensors were installed in the carpool lanes of this stretch of highway. The sensors allowed onboard computers to control the steering and speed of the two cars.

An inventor in Denmark named Palle Jensen came up with a unique idea that he calls the RUF, or Rapid, Urban, and Flexible. The RUF creates a sort of personal, individualized train system. First, travelers would get their personal electric vehicles out of their garages where they had been recharging all night. They would then drive to a nearby RUF station. There, the travelers would enter their destination into a computer, at which point the computer would take control of the vehicles. The individual vehicles would merge onto an elevated guideway and join other electronic vehicles in a small train formation. The RUF would average about 62 miles per hour (100 km/h) and would slow at certain points to let others enter and exit the guideway. Since the system would be fully automated, drivers could read, study, make phone calls, or even nap during the trip. The computer would be at the wheel most of the time, rather than the driver.

The idea of computer-controlled cars is not that far-fetched. A great many motor vehicles manufactured today have computer chips in them to perform one function or another. Experts believe that automation like that featured in the RUF system could double or even triple the number of vehicles on the road.

Optimization

A similar idea is one that is called optimization, which involves making the most of all available modes of transportation. Under this kind of system, people would plot their journey on the Internet, entering important information such as where they wanted to go, how much they wanted to spend getting there, how soon they needed to leave, and when they wanted to arrive. The computer would figure out the best combination of transportation to get them there within the time frame and cost specified. One day, the computer might recommend taking a bus and a taxi. The next time, perhaps due to different traffic patterns or an increase in taxi fares, the computer might advise taking a bus and train instead. This system would shift most people over to some form of mass transit, reducing the amount of pollution and congestion on the nation's highways.

The future activities of the DOT will change greatly and be determined by new inventions that move people from one place to another more quickly and smoothly, hopefully at less cost to travelers and to the environment. The department's main duties, however, will not change, no matter how futuristic our transportation system becomes. The DOT will always be primarily concerned with guaranteeing that Americans and American products get where they are going safely and successfully.

Conclusion

I n the twentieth century, the world's people suddenly became very mobile, able to cross the globe in a matter of hours rather than months or years. This increased mobility is likely only to increase in the future. As time goes by, the vehicles that take people where they want to go will change dramatically. No matter what kind of vehicle American travelers board, however, the Department of Transportation is sure to be there for the ride, making sure it goes as smoothly as possible.

While most people take transportation for granted, they are often unaware of all the hard work and planning that go into making modern methods of travel safe and efficient. Color-coded traffic lights are often overlooked. Only when they are not working for some reason, like during a blackout,

Stranded commuters walk over the Queensborough Bridge in New York City on August 14, 2003. A massive blackout that affected large swaths of the eastern United States and Canada resulted in ineffective traffic lights, snarled traffic, stalled trains and subways, and grounded airplanes.

do we realize how important they are to smooth and orderly traffic flow. Helpful signs, warning signals, and painted boundary lines also keep traffic flowing, even if drivers no longer consciously notice them. Speed limits and security checks at airports might sometimes seem like obstacles that only slow us down, but they are, in fact, useful tools that help ensure we get to our destinations without any tragic accidents or incidents preventing a safe arrival. Some new practices, like automated ticketing, electronic toll paying, and airport monorail systems, shorten the time and hassle of traveling, without costing anything extra to the traveler in terms of money, time,

The E-Z Pass automated toll collection system begins its first day of operation on the New Jersey side of the George Washington Bridge on July 28, 1997. E-Z Pass speeds drivers' passage through tollbooths by taking cash, coins, and toll tickets out of the toll collection process. Instead, drivers prepay tolls and attach a small electronic device to their vehicles. Tolls are automatically calculated and deducted from the prepaid accounts as E-Z Pass customers pass through the toll lanes.

or energy. All of these DOT-related activities and practices make the world of travel smoother, safer, easier, and faster.

No one is sure exactly where the future will take the human race. Without a doubt, however, whether people are traveling in the air, on the ground, or even under the water, the DOT will be there to make sure the rules are being followed, the regulations are routinely updated, and people are safely getting exactly where they want to go.

TIMELINE

October 15, 1966	The Department of Transportation is established by an act of Congress and signed into law by President Lyndon B. Johnson.
January 16, 1967–January 20, 1969	Alan S. Boyd
January 31, 1967	The DOT issues its first twenty federal motor vehicle safety standards.
June 6, 1967	The National Traffic Safety Agency and the National Highway Safety Agency merge to become the National Highway Safety Bureau.
July 1, 1968	The Urban Mass Transportation Administration is established.
January 22, 1969–February 2, 1973	John A. Volpe
September 11, 1970	President Richard M. Nixon orders the DOT to lead the government's anti-hijacking program.
October 13, 1970	President Nixon signs the Federal Railroad Safety Act, increasing the DOT's role in overseeing the safe operation of the nation's railroads.
October 15, 1970	President Nixon signs into law the Urban Mass Transportation Assistance Act, a $10 billion program designed to upgrade the nation's mass transit systems.

October 30, 1970 | Congress passes the National Railroad Passenger Safety Act, creating Amtrak.

December 31, 1970 | The DOT's National Highway Traffic Safety Administration is established.

March 9, 1972 | The Transportation Safety Institute is established.

January 5, 1973 | The FAA begins preboarding electronic screening of all passengers and inspection of their carry-on baggage.

February 2, 1973–February 1, 1975 | Claude S. Brinegar

April 5, 1974 | In response to the Arab oil embargo and resulting energy crisis, all states comply with the federal government's order to reduce maximum highway speed limits to 55 miles per hour (89 km/h).

December 13, 1974 | Still in the midst of an energy crisis, the DOT launches a nationwide campaign to encourage carpooling.

February 2, 1975–March 6, 1975 | John W. Barnum

March 7, 1975–January 20, 1977 | William T. Coleman Jr.

January 23, 1977–July 20, 1979 | Brockman "Brock" Adams

June 6, 1977 | Adams announces new fuel economy standards that should result in smaller and lighter cars. Four days later, he institutes regulations that, by 1984, will require all new cars to have either air bags or automatic seat belts.

September 23, 1977 | The Research and Special Programs Administration is established.

November 6, 1978 | The Surface Transportation Assistance Act is signed into law, consolidating federal financial assistance programs for highways and public transportation.

July 21, 1979–August 14, 1979 | W. Graham Clayton Jr.

August 15, 1979–January 20, 1981 Neil E. Goldschmidt

January 23, 1981–February 1, 1983 Andrew L. "Drew" Lewis Jr.

August 5, 1981 President Ronald Reagan fires almost 13,000 striking air traffic controllers.

December 29, 1981 President Reagan signs into law the Federal Aid Highway Act, which provides funds for the resurfacing, restoring, and reconstructing of the interstate highway system.

February 7, 1983–September 30, 1987 Elizabeth H. Dole

October 13, 1983 Secretary Dole orders the installation of eye-level brake lights on rear windows of new cars.

July 17, 1984 President Reagan signs into law legislation that establishes the national minimum drinking age at twenty-one. This is designed in part to cut down on drunk-driving deaths. States that do not comply with the new law will lose their federal highway funds.

October 1, 1987–January 30, 1989 James H. Burnley IV

February 6, 1989–December 13, 1991 Samuel K. Skinner

February 25, 1990 Smoking is banned on almost all domestic airline flights. The only exceptions are flights to Alaska or Hawaii that last more than six hours.

December 14, 1991–February 23, 1992 James B. Busey IV

February 24, 1992–January 20, 1993 Andrew H. Card Jr.

January 21, 1993–February 14, 1997 Federico F. Peña

February 3, 1994 The DOT issues alcohol and drug testing rules for more than 7 million employees who perform safety-sensitive jobs within the transportation industry.

April 21, 1994 The Office of Motor Carrier Safety launches its Share the Road campaign, designed to teach motorists how to drive more safely on highways also traveled by large trucks.

January 1, 1996 The Surface Transportation Board is established.

February 14, 1997–January 20, 2001 Rodney E. Slater

January 21, 2001–January 24, 2001 Mortimer L. Downey

January 25, 2001– Norman Y. Mineta

September 11, 2001 Al Qaeda terrorists hijack four American commercial jets and crash them into the World Trade Center in New York City, the Pentagon in Arlington, Virginia, and a field in Shanksville, Pennsylvania.

November 19, 2001 President George W. Bush signs the Aviation and Transportation Security Act into law. This creates the DOT's Transportation Security Administration, which is charged with increasing security at airports, train stations, and other major transportation centers.

March 1, 2003 The new Department of Homeland Security takes over the U.S. Coast Guard and the Transportation Security Administration from the DOT.

November 30, 2004 George W. Bush signs the Norman Y. Mineta Research and Special Programs Improvement Act. The act reorganizes the Research and Special Programs Administration of the DOT into a pipeline and hazardous materials safety administration and research organization.

bill A draft of a law presented to a legislature and submitted to a vote.

cabinet A council of the chief advisers of a head of state.

cabinet-level department A government office headed by a key adviser to a head of state, such as the president of the United States.

domestically produced oil Oil produced within U.S. borders.

economy The flow of money within a country, state, region, city, town, or household.

embargo A cutting off of trade.

federal government The central governing authority in a nation made up of several states or territories.

infrastructure The support system of a city or country that allows it to function, such as the sanitation system, power plants, water pipelines, bridges, tunnels, highways, and railways.

legislation Proposed rules created by a decision-making body.

Organization of Petroleum Exporting Countries (OPEC) A cartel of major oil-exporting countries established in 1960 to control the pricing and production of oil. In 2002, more than 77 percent of the world's proven oil reserves lay under the soil of OPEC member nations.

statistics Information that is collected, counted, analyzed, and presented publicly; information that is collected so understanding of a certain issue can be increased.

transportation The means of traveling from one place to another.

Bureau of Transportation Statistics
400 7th Street SW
Room 3103
Washington, DC 20590
Web site: http://www.bts.gov

Federal Aviation Administration
800 Independence Avenue SW
Washington, DC 20591
Web site: http://www.faa.gov

Federal Highway Administration
400 7th Street SW
Washington, DC 20590
Web site: http://www.fhwa.dot.gov

Federal Railroad Administration
1120 Vermont Avenue NW
Washington, DC 20590
Web site: http://www.fra.dot.gov

Surface Transportation Board
1925 K Street NW
Washington, DC 20423
Web site: http://www.stb.dot.gov

U.S. Department of Transportation
400 7th Street SW
Washington, DC 20590
Web site: http://www.dot.gov

WEB SITES
Due to the changing nature of
Internet links, the Rosen Publishing
Group, Inc., has developed an
online list of Web sites related to
the subject of this book. This site is
updated regularly. Please use this
link to access the list:

http://www.rosenlinks.com/tyg/tran

FOR FURTHER READING

Beyer, Mark. *Transportation of the Future*. New York, NY: Children's
    Press, 2002.

Feinberg, Barbara Silberdick. *Words in the News: A Student's Dictionary
    of American Government and Politics*. New York, NY: Franklin Watts,
    Inc., 1993.

Horn, Geoffrey M. *Cabinet and Federal Agencies*. Milwaukee, WI: Gareth
    Stevens Publishers, 2003.

Staff of Ferguson Publishing. *Transportation: Discover Careers for Your Future*.
    New York, NY: Ferguson Publishing, 2001.

Stephany, Wallace. *Department of Transportation: Know Your Government*.
    Broomall, PA: Chelsea House Publishers, 1988.

Wellman, Sam. *The Cabinet*. Broomall, PA: Chelsea House Publishers, 2001.

BIBLIOGRAPHY

Ashley, Steven. "Smart Cars and Automated Highways." Mechanical Engineering Online. 1998. Retrieved December 2003 (http://www.memagazine.org/backissues/may98/features/smarter/smarter.html).

Bourne, Russell. *Americans on the Move: A History of Waterways, Railways, and Highways*. Golden, CO: Fulcrum Publishing, 1995.

"Buck Rogers, Watch Out!" Science@NASA. March 1, 2001. Retrieved May 2004 (http://science.nasa.gov/headlines/y2001/ast01mar_1.htm).

"A Chronology of Significant DOT Dates." U.S. Department of Transportation. 2003. Retrieved December 2003 (http://isweb.tasc.dot.gov/Historian/chronology.htm).

"A Conversation with Inventor Palle Jensen." CNN.com. Retrieved December 2003 (http://www.cnn.com/interactive/tech/0103/ruf.box/content.html).

Grinder, R. Dale. "The United States Department of Transportation: A Brief History." U.S. Department of Transportation. 2003. Retrieved December 2003 (http://isweb.tasc.dot.gov/Historian/history.htm).

Lewis, Tom. *Divided Highways: Building the Interstate Highways, Transforming American Life*. New York, NY: Penguin USA, 1999.

Onion, Amanda. "The Way We'll Move." ABCNews.com. February 19, 2003. Retrieved December 2003 (http://abcnews.go.com/sections/scitech/DailyNews/futureoftransportation020219.html).

Whitnah, Donald R. *The U.S. Department of Transportation*. Westport, CT: The Greenwood Publishing Group, 1998.

INDEX

ABOUT THE AUTHOR

Tamra Orr is a full-time writer living in the Pacific Northwest. She has authored more than thirty nonfiction books for children and families, as well as countless magazine articles. She and her husband have four children, and she is sure that after researching and writing this book, she will never take transportation for granted again.

PHOTO CREDITS

Front cover (top) courtesy of Chris Lattner; front cover (portraits) U.S. Transportation Department Photo; back cover (top), pp. 3 (bottom left), 4 (circle), 4–5 (center right), 6–7, 40 © Business and Occupations/PhotoDisc; front and back cover (bottom), p. 43 © Industry and Technology/DigitalVision; p. 3 (bottom right) © Rich Bourgerie, Oceanographer, CO-OPS, NOS, NOAA; p. 12 © NARA; p. 14 © David Handschuh/AP/Wide World Photos; p. 19 © Bobby Ratliff/KCRG TV 9/AP/Wide World Photos; p. 22 © Scout Tufankjian/AP/Wide World Photos; p. 26 © Time Life Pictures/Getty Images; p. 29 © Tim Wright/Corbis; p. 31 © Neemah Aaron/AP/Wide World Photos; p. 35 © Timothy Boyl/AP/Wide World Photos; p. 37 © Timothy Jacobsen/AP/Wide World Photos; p. 42 © Jason Plotkin/The York Dispatch/AP/Wide World Photos; p. 47 © Chiaki Tsukumo/AP/Wide World Photos; p. 50 © Denis Poroy/AP/Wide World Photos; p. 53 © Sean M. Thompson/AP/Wide World Photos; p. 54 © Michael Sypniewski/AP/Wide World Photos.

Designer: Evelyn Horovicz; Photo Researcher: Hillary Arnold